The Wake We Leave

Redefining Leadership Through Humanity and Heart

By Kim Eckels

Dedication

To my husband, thank you for believing in me every step of the way, and for being my rock through it all.

To my parents, you were my first teachers in both business and life. Your example shaped the leader I've become.

To Chris Toth, thank you for showing me what true leadership looks like, with compassion, authenticity, and the courage to be human.

To Zino Lappas, your wisdom, trust, and ability to let others lead have been a masterclass in humility and strength.

Introduction: Rising Up, Speaking out, and Leading Differently

For over 20 years, I've worked in service-related roles, mostly the kind people tend to overlook or undervalue. I've spent the better part of my career being "just a" something: just a rep, just support, just customer service. I've worked under sadistic managers, witnessed toxic behaviors go unchecked, and seen far too many good people burned out, shut down, or pushed out. I've been bullied, harassed, let go, and spoken to in ways no human deserves. I've seen what happens when power is abused, and people are treated like parts in a machine.

But I also made a decision.

I decided that if I wanted to change the system, I had to rise within it. I earned my bachelor's degree. Then my master's. Not because I needed the letters after my name, but because I needed a seat at the table, and a voice that carried. I did it so I could help people like me. So, I could advocate for those who don't feel seen. So, I could challenge the systems that were never designed for us to succeed. And now that I'm in a leadership role, I've made it my mission to lead differently.

I believe in leading with kindness, balance, and humanity. I believe in creating a cultural wake, one that ripples through the organization and says: we can do better. We must do better.

This book isn't just a collection of stories; it's a call to action. I'll share moments from my own journey, some hard, some hopeful, all real. I'll show what it looks like to lead with compassion, even when the decisions aren't easy. Because leadership isn't about always getting it right. It's about showing up with integrity. It's about how you treat people, how you deliver hard news, and how you make space for others to grow, even if that growth takes them somewhere else.

We don't need more leaders who play the part. We need more leaders who live the part. And it starts with choosing to be a better human first.

Part I: The Unseen Harm
Chapter 1: Titles and Triage

Titles are funny things.

They're supposed to help define roles and responsibilities, but all too often, they become a ceiling. A line in the sand. A reason people are kept out of conversations, left out of meetings, or passed over for credit they deserve.

I know, because I've lived it.

The Idea That Should've Been a Turning Point

I was working at a large corporation, and for the first time in a while, I felt like I was being heard. I had an idea, a real one, with strategy, substance, and an action plan behind it. I didn't just throw out a suggestion. I built a portfolio. I brought data. I laid out how the company could implement it and why it would work.

Leadership bought in. There was genuine interest. Buzz, even. And for a moment, I thought this could be the start of something big, not just for the company, but for *me*.

Then my manager pulled me aside and said something that stopped me in my tracks:

"I'm so proud of you. I always knew you were more than just a customer service rep."

He meant it as a compliment. But it felt like a punch to the gut.

Because I *was* a customer service rep. That was my title. That was my role. And the message behind those words was clear: people in your position aren't expected to do things like this.

The Credit Grab and the Invisible Contributor

I was "partnered" with Marketing and Sales to bring the idea to life. But in reality, I was sidelined. My work was rebranded and reworded but the core and the mission remained the same.

When the program launched and the success rolled in, my name was nowhere. Not in the presentations. Not in the emails. Not in the conversations. The people with the bigger titles got the credit. And I stayed behind my screen, still *"just a* customer service rep."

That moment changed me.

I realized that in that culture, *titles won out over truth.* And if I wanted to be heard, *really* heard, I'd have to change something big.

So, I did.

The Choice to Rise
I went back to school. I earned my bachelor's degree. Then my master's. Not because I needed a credential, but because I needed a voice. I needed access. I needed people to take me seriously *before* I said something brilliant, not after.

And I didn't do it just for me. I did it for people like me. For every "just a" sitting in a role that doesn't reflect their value. For every employee who's been looked past because they didn't have the title that earned them a seat at the table.

Now that I'm in leadership, I do things differently. Radically differently.

What That Moment Taught Me
What I learned from that experience wasn't what I should have learned. The message that situation sent was: *when you have a good idea, you should probably keep it to yourself.* Because people at the top don't always care about where the idea comes from. They care about who gets the credit.

But that's the wrong message.

If I were leading in that organization back then, I wouldn't have taken credit for someone else's idea. I would've worked with them. Supported them. Coached them. I would've stood beside them in front of leadership, celebrating *them* for what they envisioned and helped build.

Because leadership is not about claiming other people's work, it's about helping them rise.

The Ripple Effect of Being Overlooked
When you steal someone's credit, when you leave them out of a success they helped create,

it doesn't just bruise their ego, it breaks their spirit.

And that break shows up in real ways:

- They stop raising their hand.

- They stop sharing their ideas.

- They start looking elsewhere.

It shows up in disengagement. It shows up in turnover. It shows up when your competitor ends up with the very person who had the answers you ignored.

And for what?

So, someone in a higher title could put another win on their résumé?

It's short-sighted. And it's a leadership failure.

If You're a Leader, Ask Yourself: Who Do You Want to Be?

Do you want to be the kind of leader who steps on your people to get ahead? Or do you want to be the kind of leader who lifts them up, celebrates them, and helps them grow?

That's strategy. That's culture. That's how you build loyalty and momentum.

Because when people feel seen, they show up. When they feel valued, they invest. When they know their voice matters, they speak up with brilliance.

But if they're treated like they don't matter, like they're "just a", they stop showing up with their full selves.

And in customer-facing roles especially, that disconnect doesn't stay behind the scenes. It shows up in every email, every call, every customer interaction. When you call a company and the rep sounds checked out, disengaged, and done, it's not an accident. That's not laziness. That's learned behavior.

That's what happens when you strip meaning from a role that already demands a lot and gets little in return.

Final Thoughts

You can hang all the motivational posters you want. You can write mission statements that talk about respect and innovation and collaboration. But unless your *actions* match your words, none of it matters.

Leadership is measured by how you treat people when no one's watching. It's measured by who you bring with you as you rise.

Titles matter, but *people* matter more.

Key Takeaway
Leadership isn't about being the loudest voice in the room, it's about making sure others feel heard.

Chapter 2: The Favoritism Filter

Having a right hand and a left hand is all fine and well, every leader needs people they trust. But there's a line. That line is crossed the moment praise, support, and opportunity become uneven. The moment the same names keep coming up for recognition while others are silently holding the team together in the background.

Favoritism might feel harmless on the surface, but it's one of the quietest, most corrosive forces in any organization. And the people on the receiving end? They *always* feel it.

The Small Office, the Golden Child, and the Fallout

I once worked for a small insurance company. Just the owner, myself, and one other person in the office. On paper, it should've been a close-knit, collaborative space. But the other woman in the office had been there for years, unofficially given the title of "office manager," and very clearly favored by the owner.

At first, I rolled with it. I made friends with her. We even spent time together outside of work. But something felt... off.

As time went on, the cracks began to show. There were days she came into work reeking of alcohol. The owner was often gone for weeks at a time, and she'd take long, unexplained absences in the middle of the day. I started noticing some highly questionable practices, especially in how she handled policies for her family. What I saw wasn't just sloppy. It was fraud.

I tried to give her the benefit of the doubt, but eventually I couldn't ignore it. I didn't want to see her fired, I genuinely believed she needed help. But I knew that without proof, nothing would happen. So, I did something I'd never done before: I recorded a conversation. I brought it to the owner, expecting at the very least that it would lead to accountability.

What I got instead was blame.

He told me I needed to "try harder to get along with her." Meanwhile, I was being bullied, my desk rifled through during lunch breaks, everything dumped on the floor. I was receiving veiled threats about walking my dog in the morning. Not overt, but just enough to make me feel unsafe.

And while I was trying to survive that nightmare, the owner responded by... buying her a car. Then moving her into one of his rental properties because her home wasn't livable.

That level of protection and kindness, I could've understood, if it wasn't tied to someone actively hurting others. Someone actively causing harm, committing fraud, and making the workplace unsafe.

I left that job. But the psychological scars ran deep. That kind of favoritism wasn't just frustrating, it was traumatizing. It sent a message that no matter what you do, no matter how right you are, the favorite wins. And the rest of us? We're disposable.

A Tale of Two Leaders

Favoritism doesn't only show up in small offices. I saw it again at a much larger company, this time between two upper-level managers. One of them was competent, thoughtful, strategic. He was there to lead, not to play politics. The other? He was completely incompetent. His decisions created chaos, his focus was on appearances and career climbing, and he didn't care about the people under him, at all.

I was working closely with the good manager, helping to design and build out a new team. We had something strong. But the other manager, let's just say he got involved where he shouldn't have. He told an entire team that they were being reassigned, moved into different roles, none of which was true.

I was in those meetings. I knew what had actually been decided.

Still, the good manager took the fall. He gathered everyone together, looked them in the eye, and said: *"I apologize. I must have miscommunicated. That's on me."*

But it wasn't on him.

A month later, he was let go.

The other manager? Promoted. Because his last name happened to carry weight with people higher up the chain. That one decision sent a wave of defeat through the teams. People talked. Group chats filled with quiet rage. No one trusted the leadership anymore, not because of the decision alone, but because everyone *already knew* what was going on. The promotion just confirmed it.

When Favorites Cost You the Team

Favoritism isn't always loud. Sometimes, it hides in plain sight, and it can cost you your entire team if you're not paying attention.

I once stepped into a leadership role over a team that, to put it bluntly, looked like the Bad News Bears. Unstructured, underperforming, and completely off-course. But it wasn't because everyone was slacking. The problem was very specific: the favorites of the prior manager were dragging the whole team down.

These individuals had no accountability. They showed up late, left early, took long breaks, and spent most of their time on social media. Meanwhile, the truly hardworking employees were picking up the slack, and they were *burnt out*. I had team members coming to me, telling me they were ready to leave. And I believed them. They had reached the point where they no longer believed hard work mattered.

The "favorites" were indifferent to everything. One in particular made it clear from day one that they had no intention of changing. Why would they? They had been rewarded for doing the bare minimum. Being the favorite had kept them safe.

But I wasn't there to preserve comfort. I was there to lead. I introduced new rules. Clear expectations. Accountability. The favorite resisted at every turn, and eventually, we had to part ways.

That decision wasn't easy, but it was necessary. Because what was really at risk wasn't just one employee. It was *everyone else*. It was the people who cared. The people who worked late. The people who believed in the mission and wanted to make an impact.

Favoritism nearly cost me an entire team.

Leaders: sometimes you don't see the damage being done because you're too close to the person causing it. You're not seeing the missed deadlines. The eye rolls. The side conversations. The resentment building quietly in your once-engaged team.

I've seen good people leave because of favoritism. I've seen high performers check out, give up, and disappear because they no longer believed they were playing in a fair system.

And the irony? The favorite who causes the damage often isn't even your best employee. You're holding onto them out of habit. Out of familiarity. Out of comfort. Meanwhile, your actual talent is walking out the door.

The Unspoken Cost of Playing Favorites

When favoritism happens and great employees are passed over, they *feel it*. You can feel it in the room, it's heavy, unspoken, and impossible to ignore. It creates a ripple effect that, over time, can erode even the healthiest culture and turn it into a hostile, disconnected environment.

It becomes high school all over again. You've got the popular kids, and everyone else. Some team members will scramble for inclusion. Others will shrink, slowly losing their drive. Either way, it leaves people feeling invisible. And when you feel invisible long enough, you stop trying. You stop sharing. You stop caring.

Favoritism is a fast track to disengagement.

And disengagement turns into turnover. Not just any turnover, *the worst kind*: the loss of your best people. The most thoughtful. The most capable. The ones who show up, not for attention, but because they *care*. And now they're working for someone else, bringing their brilliance to a company that actually sees them.

That's what you lose when you lead with bias instead of balance.

This Isn't a One-Industry Problem
This isn't exclusive to corporate jobs or customer service roles. I've seen it in insurance, manufacturing, IT, service, and support. It shows up in companies of ten, and companies of ten thousand.

It shows up in any environment where one person gets all the praise, all the grace, all the visibility, while the rest of the team is treated like scenery.

What Real Leadership Looks Like
So how do we fix it?

We stop handpicking *favorites* and start handpicking *teams*. We coach everyone. We build individual development plans, not just for the squeaky wheels or the office socialites, but for the quiet steady ones. The ones who've been holding your business together in ways you haven't even noticed.

We give praise freely. We set expectations clearly. We measure growth honestly.

I don't care if you're leading entry-level employees or executives. Leadership is about creating an *environment*, one that's fair, inclusive, and consistent.

And no, not everyone will work the same. That's not the point.

The point is: if the culture is fair, and people are treated with equity, the whole team rises.

That's the difference between building a strong organization and managing a popularity contest.

Final Thoughts
Favoritism isn't just a bad habit, it's a leadership failure. It costs you morale. It costs

you trust. And eventually, it costs you people. When only one person feels seen, the rest feel invisible. And when people feel invisible, they start disappearing.

As a leader, your job isn't to create an inner circle. Your job is to build a circle big enough for *everyone*.

Key Takeaway: *Favoritism may feel harmless at the top, but it fractures everything underneath.*

Chapter 3: What We Don't Talk About

The Emotional and Psychological Toll of Being Overlooked

We talk about innovation, transformation, and people-first culture. We talk about engagement and inclusion. But what we don't talk about is the cost of being unseen.

What we don't talk about is how it feels to go home every day carrying the weight of silence. How it feels to be overlooked. Dismissed. Ignored. Or worse, acknowledged only when something goes wrong.

The Story Beneath the Silence

When I walk into teams, especially ones marked by dysfunction, I listen first. I observe. I look for the silent fractures in the system. And more often than not, I find them. Because they're always there. Just below the surface.

I've watched amazing employees leave. Not because they weren't engaged, not because they didn't love their job, but because the environment pushed them out. And after they leave, leadership says, *"It's a shame, we really valued them."*

No. You valued the outcome. You didn't value the person. If you had, they wouldn't have felt the need to leave.

There's a cost to toxicity. But we rarely talk about it. We make excuses for the known problem people, especially the ones who produce. We tolerate bad behavior because *"that's just how they are."* We allow trauma to live in the hallways of our offices, never naming it, never addressing it.

And when decisions from the top contradict the company's values, no one wants to speak up. Not the mid-level leaders. Not the managers. Not the employees. Because they're afraid.

Afraid of being labeled "difficult." Afraid of retaliation. Afraid of losing their job.

We say we want feedback. But we don't always create the safety required to receive it.

When Culture Contradicts Itself

It's easy to say we're a people-centered organization. But if your health plan isn't affordable, you're not people-centered. If your pay scale is below market, you're not people-centered. If your PTO policy favors executives while hourly employees are scraping by, you're not people-centered. If your surveys aren't truly anonymous, or worse, if people *don't believe* they're anonymous, you're not people-centered. You're optics-centered.

We tout culture because we want to believe it's strong. But I've been in rooms where the survey results glow green, while the real conversation in the breakroom is "don't say anything or it'll come back to you."

I've seen employees delete honest comments from surveys out of fear. I've done it myself.

We keep talking about culture, but we keep avoiding the conversations that matter.

The Cost of Being Overlooked
What happens when people don't feel seen?

They disengage. They internalize. They carry quiet wounds.

They work through birthdays, illnesses, grief, and stress, and get told, *"Thank you for being a team player."* But not, *"How are you holding up?"* Not, *"What do you need?"*

We don't talk about what it's like to be in customer service and find out about a change only after a customer calls in confused.

We don't talk about the burnout that sets in when the only feedback you receive is what went wrong, never what went right.

We don't talk about the resentment that builds when leadership is too far removed to see how hard their teams are working. Or when managers with strong character are silenced by systems that favor compliance over courage.

We don't talk about the exhaustion of always having to "act okay."

We don't talk about the fact that many of us stay silent because we *have to*. Because speaking up might cost us more than just a job, it could cost us stability, healthcare, our ability to care for our families.

So we smile. We nod. And we carry the pain home.

The Breakdown in Communication
There's another layer to the silence, one that echoes through every missed memo, last-minute rollout, and after-the-fact announcement.

It's the communication gap.

Too often, decisions are made at the top without any real understanding of how they will ripple down to the people expected to carry them out. Leadership assumes that information flows naturally. That updates will trickle down in a clean, linear fashion. But that's rarely the case.

I've worked in environments where customers knew about major changes, price increases, policy shifts, or system updates, *before* my teams did. I've had conversations where customers asked questions I couldn't answer because no one had informed us. And I've sat in leadership roles, only to find out about decisions *after* they had already been implemented.

The result? Embarrassment. Frustration. Confusion. And a breakdown in trust, not just between leadership and employees, but between employees and the customers they serve.

When people are left out of the loop, it signals that their voice doesn't matter. That their role is to execute, not contribute. That their perspective, despite being closest to the front line, holds no weight.

This kind of miscommunication is more than an inconvenience. It's a cultural failure.

Because every decision has stakeholders. Every system change impacts someone. And when you leave those stakeholders out of the process, you create more than inefficiency, you create stress.

Stress that builds into resentment. Stress that leads to burnout. Stress that becomes turnover. And turnover becomes cost.

Companies often talk about being "people-centered," but overlook the most basic need people have in the workplace: *to be informed*. To be included. To have a say in the systems they use every day.

If you really want to operate with empathy and excellence, you don't just announce change, you *build* it with the people it will affect. You communicate clearly, consistently, and with respect.

Because people-centered isn't just a brand statement. It's a practice. And poor communication is one of the clearest signs that the practice isn't matching the promise.

The Unspoken Violence of Workplace Bullying

There's another truth we rarely speak aloud: **Workplace bullying is real.** And it cuts deeper than most people realize.

It doesn't always look like yelling. Sometimes it's quiet, calculated exclusion. Sometimes it's humiliation dressed up as "leadership." Sometimes it's the slow erosion of your dignity, day by day, moment by moment.

Years ago, I worked in a small insurance office. I didn't know it at the time, but I was sick. I was later diagnosed with cancer. While

I was out for medical reasons, my manager demanded access to my emails. I explained, calmly and professionally, that I couldn't share my password, it was against corporate policy and tied to my insurance license.

That explanation didn't matter.

She accused me of questioning her ethics. She raised her voice. She berated me. When I returned from lunch, she micromanaged me to the point of humiliation. By the next day, I wasn't even allowed to touch my computer. I was sent home early, and then terminated.

The official reason? They were eliminating the role. The truth? She bullied me.

A month earlier, she called me "an angel sent from heaven." But that praise vanished the moment I upheld compliance.

And I've seen it happen to others too.

I've worked in companies where senior leaders stood in corners mocking employees just loud enough to be heard. I've watched good people go home in tears, wondering what they did wrong.

The answer? They said no. Or they didn't fit in. Or they simply became a target.

But these are not disposable workers. These are people. With families. With bills. With lives.

No one should have to endure bullying in any form.

If you're a leader, especially one with influence, you must never tolerate this behavior. Ever. Because it's not just happening in one place. It may not exist everywhere. But it exists in enough places that we need to stop pretending it's rare.

Because bullying thrives in silence. And silence is what we're trying to break.

If You Really Want to Lead
Then listen.

Not just with your ears, but with your heart. Look for the invisible. Pay attention to what's not being said. Create spaces where truth can breathe.

Hire managers with strength of character. Celebrate wins. Communicate clearly. Be consistent. And for the love of all things human, put your money where your mouth is.

Leadership isn't about being liked. It's about being trusted.

And trust is built when people feel safe to speak, even when what they say is hard to hear.

Because what we don't talk about is what shapes the culture the most.

Where We've Been

When I go back through the Rolodex in my mind, yes, I just said Rolodex, I can clearly picture what leadership used to look like.

It was power. Power *over* people. It was a man in an office, dictating to his secretary. It was a boardroom full of suits, making decisions behind closed doors. It was a workplace where women were undervalued, where hierarchy reigned, and where authority was measured by volume and intimidation.

Leadership was ego-driven. It lived in corner offices and gold nameplates. It showed up late, barked orders, and took credit. It fired people for being sick. It fired people for mistakes.

It was not strength. It was fear, dressed up as power.

And for too long, we accepted that version of leadership as normal.

The Wake-Up Call

It wasn't until years later that I discovered leadership could be something else entirely.

During a corporate restructuring, our company was split into a new division, and that's when I met the most impactful leader I've ever known.

Naturally, I did my research. I watched his fireside chats. Scrolled through social media. Listened between the lines.

But what I discovered wasn't a brand or a carefully curated executive persona.

I found *character*.

He didn't lead with jargon or corporate polish. He led with heart.

What struck me most was that it wasn't performative. It wasn't strategy. It was who he was.

And it changed the way I thought about leadership.

The Comparison

Before him, what I knew of the C-suite was this:

- They were untouchable.

- Surrounded by yes-men.

- Disconnected from the actual people doing the work.

- Measured success only by numbers.

- Dismissed the human cost.

But this leader was different. He showed up. He listened. He coached instead of criticized. He led with humility and made decisions with integrity, *because it was the right thing to do.*

He reminded me that the collateral damage of leadership decisions is not theoretical, it's people. People with families. People with stories. People who deserve compassion.

What It Means to Lead with Kindness
Leadership rooted in kindness feels different. It honors the whole person. It recognizes the layers of life outside the workplace. It creates space for connection, growth, and healing.

I've led employees through illness, grief, burnout, and moments of deep personal struggle.

And I've watched how a single act of compassion, a check-in, a flexible deadline, a willingness to listen, can turn someone from surviving to thriving.

It doesn't work with everyone. But it works with many.

And like toxicity, kindness spreads.

The Myth of Softness
People often mistake kindness for weakness.

They assume compassionate leaders are pushovers. That kindness means you won't make tough calls. That empathy dilutes authority.

But the truth is: **Kindness is power.**

It takes more strength to lead with compassion than it does to lead with fear. It takes courage to be transparent. To hold space. To admit when you're wrong. To care, even when it's inconvenient.

You don't have to be everyone's best friend.
But you *can* be kind.

And still be respected. And still be decisive.
And still lead powerfully.

When Fear Poses as Leadership

I've known leaders who believe in ruling with
an iron fist. "I want them to know who's
boss," they say.

But they're not leading. They're controlling.

I watched one such leader humiliate
employees in meetings, pointing fingers,
yelling, twisting facts, blaming everyone else.

That's not leadership. That's fear in disguise.

And fear is not a sustainable business strategy.

True leadership connects. It inspires. It *leads
people forward*, not drives them down.

So What Do We Do?

We pause.

When mistakes happen, when tempers rise, pause. Take five seconds. Count.

And then ask yourself:

What would have helped *me* when I was the one who messed up?

Was it shouting? Or was it support?

We are all human. We all make mistakes. We all have lives beyond the inbox.

Kindness isn't about letting everything slide. It's about seeing the full picture, and responding with both accountability and care.

What People Want
Most people want to feel:

- Seen

- Heard

- Respected

They want to be treated like they matter. Because they *do*.

So walk around. Learn names. Check in. Share what you can. Be human.

Even five minutes of connection can make a lasting impact.

Yes, you're busy. We all are.

But people remember how you made them feel.

And if you want to build a team that trusts you, start with kindness.

The Shift We Need
It's not 1952 anymore.

We are done with leadership models rooted in fear. We are done with screaming, bullying, and power trips.

That's not strength. That's insecurity in a suit.

True strength is connection. True power is compassion. True leadership is human.

Chapter 5: Listening as Leadership

Active Listening as a Leadership Tool

More Than Words: What It Means to Be Heard.

There have been only a handful of times in my career when I didn't just feel *listened to*, I felt *heard*. There's a distinction. One acknowledges your voice. The other validates your experience.

One of the most powerful moments of being heard came when I reached out to a new CEO who had just come on board. I wasn't in a high-ranking position. I didn't expect much. I simply had ideas, big ones, and a desire to understand who he was. So, I sent him a carefully crafted email asking for a meeting. When I told a coworker what I'd done, she warned me: *Don't expect a quick response. These people with big titles don't reply quickly, especially to people at our level.*

But that same day, he responded. He didn't want to meet virtually. He wanted to meet in person. He appreciated the courage it took to reach out. And in that meeting, something extraordinary happened.

Presence Over Power

I walked in with a list of business ideas. That's just who I am. I like to come prepared. But as I nervously began to speak, he gently interrupted and said, *"I just want to know who you are."*

No one in leadership had ever asked me that.

Within minutes, we were talking about my cancer journey. He shared his mother's battle. He didn't look through me. He didn't check his watch. He looked me in the eye. He listened, not just to my words, but to what was underneath them.

That one conversation changed the way I thought about leadership. Because when someone in power listens to you like you matter, *you start to believe that you do.* I left that meeting energized. Validated. Seen. And I've carried his words with me since the day I left that company: *Be yourself. Stay true to who you are. That's what's going to take you far.*

When Listening is Absent

Not all experiences have been that healing. That same organization was riddled with contradictions, stated values that weren't lived out. My direct manager was mostly indifferent. I worked 12-hour days, often 6-7 days a week. Burnout was setting in hard, and nothing about the culture made it feel safe to raise my hand and say, *I'm drowning.*

He may have seen it, but he didn't *recognize* it. He certainly didn't address it.

And this wasn't the first time I felt unseen at work.

The Unseen Patterns
Years ago, in the insurance world, I worked in an office where the manager turned into a tyrant the moment the owner left. She would berate staff over being one minute late, all while closing her office door each afternoon to secretly drink vodka. Everyone knew something was off, but when I privately raised concerns, I was told to stay in my lane.

When she finally retired, she openly admitted to the daily drinking and shoe shopping behind closed doors. That revelation stung, not because I wanted to be right, but because it proved that those of us trying to protect the environment had been right all along. But we were dismissed.

At another agency, I reported that an office manager was making greeting cards during work hours. Again, I was brushed off.

But the worst? That came when I sold an insurance policy to a new neighbor who turned out to be a nightmare. She filed false complaints about me "partying" on the weekends. The truth? We were a group of quiet, card-playing 20-somethings listening to Kenny Rogers and sipping drinks, not exactly wild.

She took pictures through my window. My manager berated me in front of others, called me names, told me I was an embarrassment to the company. Only later, after talking to the client's former agency, did the truth come out, this woman had a history of doing this to office workers. But the damage had been done. The humiliation stuck. I left soon after.

At a different agency that *did* hear me and valued my contributions, I became number one in the region for life insurance sales.

The Ripple Effect of Being Ignored

The trauma that comes from being unseen or dismissed is real. It chips away at your confidence and self-worth. It creates a quiet tsunami beneath the surface that can impact your mental health, productivity, and sense of belonging.

If you want a disengaged workforce, ignore them. If you want the bare minimum, make people feel like they're a problem instead of a possibility. But if you want greatness? Listen. Create a culture of consistent, open, *active listening*.

What Active Listening Really Is

Active listening isn't passive. It's not just nodding or pretending to care. It's being present.

It's not:

- Thinking about your response while the other person is speaking.

- Entering the conversation with a fixed judgment or bias.

- Using your title as a shield against feedback.

- Shifting blame when something falls through the cracks.

It *is*:

- Repeating back what you heard.

- Validating the person's experience, even if you don't agree with it.

- Creating space for them to speak honestly without fear.

- Following through on action items when the conversation ends.

Active listening is the foundation of psychological safety, and that's the soil where trust grows.

Training and Accountability
Every company, big or small, should have mandatory training on active listening. It doesn't have to break the budget. It could be a LinkedIn course, a podcast series, or a well-curated audiobook. But it should be mandatory. It should be embedded in leadership development. Because when leaders don't know how to listen, they won't know how to lead.

I once had a training manager whose personal life interfered with the flow of our program. We didn't finish all the material. Later, when I didn't know something that had supposedly been covered, I was told the box had been checked, so it must have been taught. Instead of investigating, they blamed.

That wasn't just a knowledge gap. It was a failure of leadership. And that failure could have been avoided through one simple tool: *listening.*

The Wake We Leave
The wake we leave behind as leaders isn't shaped by our PowerPoint decks or our quarterly numbers. It's shaped by how we show up for people. How we see them. How we hear them.

So listen to your people. Don't assume. Ask. Create safe space. Follow through. Show up. And when you're tempted to dismiss, to judge, or to rush to the next task, pause, and remember:

Your greatest leadership tool is not in your title. It's in your ability to truly hear the human sitting across from you.

Chapter 6: The Wake You Leave

The Question That Changed Everything

I was asked in an interview once, *"What was your proudest moment in your career?"*

It only took a second for my answer to rise: it wasn't a project I led, a target I hit, or a recognition I received. It was the people. The individuals I helped grow into new roles, the ones I encouraged when they didn't yet see their own potential. That's the kind of legacy I want to leave behind.

I don't want to be remembered by my title. I don't want my name etched into a door or remembered for how I moved up the ladder. I want to be remembered as someone who **cared**. Someone who **believed** in people. Someone who created a safe place for others to grow. A leader who left behind a wake of **transformation**, not fear.

Why Are You Leading?
That's the question. That's the one we don't ask often enough.

Why are you leading?

Is it for power? For control? For a polished résumé? If your answer is anything other than *to serve and uplift others,* you're in the wrong seat.

This isn't the military. It's not a life-or-death operation. This is business. It's an office. A team. A group of human beings trying to navigate the pressures of life and work with some semblance of purpose and peace.

It doesn't matter if that team is made up of customer service reps, analysts, doctors, lawyers, or engineers. Your role is to **guide** them, not to rule over them.

And let's be honest, yes, some industries are intensely focused on performance metrics, sales targets, billable hours, and bottom lines. But **you can have excellence without abuse**. You can lead with strength and still be kind. You can win without leaving a trail of burnout behind you.

Leadership is not about pounding fists. It's about steady hands.

The Ripple or the Wreckage

So ask yourself, who do you want to be remembered as?

Do you want to be remembered as the unstable tyrant who left behind a wake of fear and disengagement?

Or do you want to be remembered as the ripple, a force that moved quietly but powerfully, creating lasting positive change in every direction?

That's the wake we leave. It doesn't come from a job title. It comes from how we show up, how we listen, how we lead.

And yes, you can assess that impact now. In fact, you should.

The Leader's Mirror
When I step into a new role, one of my first priorities is to evaluate my impact, and begin understanding the landscape of the team I'm inheriting. That starts with something simple but powerful: questions.

I create a short list and schedule one-on-one conversations. I ask about hobbies, favorite parts of their role, and where they want to grow. Why hobbies? Because they reveal what drives a person. Someone who loves cooking or gaming is often motivated by mastery. Someone deeply involved with family might be driven by relationships. Others may light up when they talk about accolades or competition, indicating external motivators.

Knowing this gives me tools to lead more effectively. Because the truth is, **not everyone responds to the same type of leadership.**

Throughout my career, I've developed a *polyblend* of **transformational and situational leadership.** I lead with vision, but I adapt with care. I don't believe in treating everyone the same, I believe in treating everyone **fairly**, according to what brings out their best.

Evaluate the Wake You Leave
Want to know the kind of wake you're leaving right now?

Here are the questions that matter, and they go deeper than KPIs.

1. People Growth & Empowerment
Have people grown under your leadership? Are your employees psychologically safe and empowered?

Look at the signs:

- Are high performers staying, or are they leaving?

- Are people being promoted from within your team?

- Are responsibilities increasing because of trust and competence?

- Do people come to you for feedback and mentorship?

If the answer to these is *yes,* you're likely empowering, not micromanaging.

2. *Culture & Emotional Climate*
How does your presence make people feel? More importantly, how does your **absence** make them feel?

Are people relaxed and collaborative, or are they guarded and competitive?

- Does morale shift when you walk into the room?

- Do smiles fade, conversations die, energy shrink?

- Are you witnessing healthy collaboration, or a Hunger Games dynamic?

- Are complaints frequent, or is there peace and accountability?

Your presence should energize. Not suppress.

3. Business Results
Of course, leadership includes outcomes. But the numbers only tell part of the story.

- Have your team's KPIs improved?

- Is customer satisfaction up?

- Has innovation increased under your watch?

- Have you successfully led your team through change or challenge?

Happier teams **are** higher-performing teams. The best results happen when people feel safe, heard, and seen.

4. Legacy & Influence
If you left tomorrow, what would happen?

- Would there be a gap?

- Are your leadership practices being adopted by others?

- Are you part of succession conversations?

- Do people seek you out for insight, mentorship, or difficult decisions?

The strongest legacies aren't loud, they're *felt* in rooms you're not even in.

5. Self-Reflection & Integrity
This is where it gets personal.

- Are you proud of how you lead, even on your worst day?

- Do you make decisions aligned with your values, even when it's hard?

- Have you taken feedback and grown from it?

- Do you act with integrity even when no one is watching?

You don't need a journal to reflect, but it helps. Even just five minutes at the end of the day to ask: *Was I the kind of leader today that I would want to follow?*

That question can change everything.

The Culture You Create
Understand this: the wake you leave isn't just personal, it's organizational.

When you build a culture of trust, growth, and accountability, you're not just shaping your team. You're shaping the **entire company**. People stay when they feel seen. They perform when they feel supported. They speak up when they feel safe.

And when you lead with compassion and courage, you earn something more powerful than compliance, you earn **respect**. Not just as a leader. As a human.

Part III: The Leader's Path Forward
Chapter 7: The Mirror Test

Raised for the Back Office, Built for the Boardroom

I was raised to be a secretary.

It's ironic, really, because my mom, although I didn't realize it at the time, was the unnamed CEO of my parents' business. She ran the operations. She made things happen. But still, the messaging I received growing up was clear: respect authority, defer to the title, and understand your place in the hierarchy. Businessmen were important. Doctors knew best. The person whose name was on the door was never to be questioned.

That type of thinking becomes deeply ingrained. And for a long time, I held one of the most limiting beliefs a future leader can carry: that those with titles knew everything.

The Myth of the All-Knowing Leader
Let me be very honest, I don't know everything. In my current role, I can't enter orders. I can't perform every piece of the day-

to-day operations. And that's okay. Because I have incredibly capable people on my team who do.

They coach. They support. They train. They are the heartbeat of the operation. And my role is to support *them*, not to pretend I'm the expert in everything.

I had to unlearn the idea that leadership requires omniscience. It doesn't. What it requires is humility, curiosity, and the ability to trust and empower others.

The Lunchroom Rebellion
Early in one leadership role, I inherited a team that was operating without structure. People clocked in from the parking lot. Others clocked out from home. Everyone disappeared at lunch, almost all at the same time. It wasn't sustainable, and it wasn't accountable.

Coming from a call center background, I created a simple policy: no more than two people at lunch at once. I thought it was reasonable.

But what I didn't know, and what the team graciously pointed out to me, is that this team didn't get many calls. Their workload was almost entirely email-driven. They weren't all needed at their desks to maintain service levels. Their pushback wasn't defensive, it was constructive.

And I listened.

I adapted the guideline. I allowed the group to have input. And it worked better than anything I would have written on my own.

That's the point.

You can lead with intention and still get it wrong. And if you're open to feedback, if you listen, you can get it right again.

The Chinks in the Armor

I didn't fully understand this truth until I lived it.

As an employee, I began to see the cracks in the facade. I started to notice that some leaders weren't as flawless as I'd believed. But the most eye-opening moment came when a manager, right before leaving the company, opened up completely.

They spilled everything, about the dysfunction, the mistakes, the lack of direction from senior leadership. Their honesty stunned me. Not because of what they shared, but because I realized something profound:

They didn't have it all figured out.

They were tired. Burned out. Doing their best in a chaotic environment.

And that's when it really sank in, no one, no matter their title, has all the answers.

Not even me.

And that's okay.

Creating Space for Growth
So how do we create a space to grow?

How do we dismantle the hard-coded beliefs that hold us back?

For me, it starts with observation. I'm a chronic observer. I don't just run meetings, I read the room. I feel the energy. If three people are laughing and the rest are silent, I don't ignore it, I investigate it. Because silence is often louder than words.

Leadership is about noticing. And growth happens in those quiet, uncomfortable moments.

It takes strength to admit you're wrong. It takes courage to change course. And it takes wisdom to know when to listen instead of lead.

When It's Hard to Look

It's easy to look in the mirror when everything's going right.

But what about when it's not?

That's the real test of leadership, when things start falling apart. When pressure mounts. When decisions are questioned. When the result isn't what you wanted.

How do you respond?

Do you look for someone to blame to take the heat off yourself? Do you get defensive or frustrated? Do you wear it on your face before a word even leaves your mouth?

I'll admit something here: I'm a highly transparent person. I don't always hold my cards close. My energy shifts. My face says what my words don't. And my team knows it. They know when I'm not okay, and most of the time, it has nothing to do with them.

If it *is* something they did, I can have that conversation calmly and constructively. But when it's something happening outside our team, something I can't control, that's when my emotions show up. And you know what? That's okay too.

What matters is the space we've created.

The space where *I* can say to my team, "Hey, is everything okay?" and they can say it right back to me. I've had team members check in, tell me they've noticed my energy is off, or ask if something's going on. That kind of mutual vulnerability only happens when psychological safety is real, not just a buzzword.

Being vulnerable with your team is part of leadership. Admitting you don't have all the answers. Owning that you need a moment to think something through. That's not incompetence, that's self-awareness. And it opens the door to collaboration, connection, and trust.

Because here's the truth: Just because you're the leader doesn't mean you're the only one with insight.

Sometimes your team knows things you don't. Sometimes *they* are the ones with the answer. So ask them. Lean on them. Respect them.

And please, never reduce them to *just a.*

Just a coordinator. Just an admin. Just a tech. Just a rep.

They're not *just* anything. They are the living, breathing engine of your organization. They are decision-makers, problem-solvers, and experts in their own right, inside and outside of work.

Their wisdom may not come with a title, but it matters. Their ideas may not come with a presentation, but they're powerful.

The Mirror Test
So ask yourself:

- **Am I the kind of leader I would want to work for?**

- **Am I treating people the way I want to be treated?**

- **Am I listening, or just talking?**

- **Am I operating from fear, ego, or empathy?**

- **What belief or bias do I need to unlearn?**

And maybe the hardest question of all:

Have I given myself the grace to grow?

Because that's part of leadership too.

Leadership isn't about knowing everything. It's about being willing to learn, unlearn, and relearn. It's about reflection, self-awareness, and a relentless pursuit of better.

So take a breath. Give yourself a moment.

And look in the mirror.

Now ask yourself, do I like what I see? Would I be motived by a leader like me?

Chapter 8: Building Better Systems

Moving from people-dependent to principle-centered leadership.

Titles come and go. Leaders come and go. But systems, that's what lasts. The infrastructure we build, or fail to build, becomes the invisible scaffolding that either holds a team up or keeps pulling it down. And here's the hard truth: the greatest leadership in the world will only take you so far if the systems don't support it.

But building those systems takes more than knowing process maps or org charts. It takes vision. It takes heart. And sometimes, it takes building with what you have, not what you wish you had.

Start Where You Are

Not every company is going to invest in the perfect training program. Not every company is going to give you the right metrics, the right software, or the ideal team. So you have to get scrappy. You have to get creative. You have to *build from within.*

One of the first things I do when leading a team is look at how knowledge is shared. Is it organized? Accessible? Or is it all locked in someone's head? Because if a team is underperforming, more often than not, it's not about will, it's about structure.

Does your company rely on tribal knowledge? Do SOPs exist? If they do, are they up to date? How do people find answers to the questions they have? How long does it take them to get the information they need to do their job well?

If those systems don't exist, or if they're broken, then that's where the work begins.

The Department That Time Forgot

Years ago, I was brought into a company after they'd made the mistake of annexing an entire department. Everyone in that department had 10–15 years of experience, but no documentation. No policies. No procedures. Nothing. It was all in their heads. The company, in its infinite wisdom, thought the department wasn't necessary, until they realized how wrong they were.

That's when I came in.

They asked me to rebuild the function from scratch, but with just three hybrid employees splitting their time between two roles. It didn't take long to see that the coverage wasn't enough. But we didn't have the metrics to prove it, because the existing metrics only showed a fraction of the work. The real workload? Buried in personal inboxes.

So we started documenting everything. Every question, every answer, every step. We didn't want to ask the same thing twice or lose time chasing ghosts. We built knowledge documents and SOPs from the ground up. We created a centralized knowledge site. Then we built the case for more staffing, and got it.

That knowledge site didn't just make onboarding easier; it *cut training time from months to weeks.*

And we didn't stop there. We also restructured the training itself. The first wave of training wasn't effective, so we pivoted. We assigned a training lead. We partnered new hires with experienced staff. We identified what worked and left behind what didn't. And when I left, one of those original team members was promoted into my role.

That's the kind of system that sustains itself. That's what it means to build something that lasts beyond you.

Growth Is Not a Buzzword

Now, let's talk about growth, and let's be honest about it. In too many organizations, "development opportunities" are code for *more work, no pay.* A pat on the back, maybe. A new title? Rare. A raise? Don't hold your breath.

That's not growth. That's exploitation.

Real growth includes upward mobility. Real growth means if you're going to expand someone's role or give them new responsibilities, there's recognition, compensation, and a clear path forward.

If your team structure doesn't allow for that, change it.

You can:

- Tier roles (Tier I, II, III)

- Create hybrid lanes that bridge customer service and IT, inside sales, or project management

- Identify cross-functional skills and design roles around them

- Build in mentorship and leadership tracks that *don't* require someone to become a manager if that's not their path

Not everyone wants to be a supervisor. But most people want to grow. They want to learn. They want to feel like their career is moving forward, not stuck on repeat. And when you design your systems around that reality, everything changes.

Equity Requires Structure

Let's talk about fairness for a minute. If a few team members are carrying the bulk of the workload while others coast through their day, that's not a people problem. That's a *systems* problem.

You can fix that by:

- Implementing ticketing or workload distribution tools

- Conducting time studies

- Creating clear metrics and benchmarks

- Tracking completion times to identify training needs

It's not about micromanaging. It's about creating a system where *everyone has an equal opportunity to contribute and succeed.*

Because equity doesn't just happen. It's built.

Recognition Should Be Structural, Too

Recognition isn't a perk. It's a pillar.

If people feel invisible, they disconnect. If they feel valued, they engage. And if they feel celebrated, they *thrive.*

Recognition needs to be:

- Tied to values and effort, not just visibility

- Shared publicly when appropriate, like when a customer sends a compliment

- Structured into your systems, not left to chance

One of the most powerful things you can do as a leader is say, *"I see you. I see what you did. And it mattered."*

Legacy Isn't a Nameplate

Here's the part nobody tells you: your legacy isn't your title. It's not how many direct reports you had. It's not even your metrics.

Your legacy is *how people feel when they think about working with you.* It's the knowledge you passed down. The growth you enabled. The fairness you modeled. The systems you built that outlasted your presence.

You don't just pass the baton. You light the way. You build a track that others can run on. You make sure no one stumbles because the system only worked for one runner.

That's how you create a legacy worth remembering.

**Cultural change doesn't require a
revolution. It begins with a whisper.
One person choosing to do the right
thing when it would be easier to look
the other way. One act of kindness
when the room feels cold. One decision
to inform, include, appreciate. One
voice. One choice. At a time.**

I've worked in many environments, some
defined by rigid hierarchy, some so loose they
lacked any real structure. I've seen thriving,
inclusive teams. I've also seen toxicity masked
as tradition. But there's one truth that applies
universally: no culture stays static. Everything
evolves. The question is, are we evolving *with
it* or *in resistance to it*?

And as leaders, we can't afford to sit back and
let culture happen *to* us. We are culture
creators. The energy we bring, the decisions
we make, the boundaries we set, or fail to set,
all shape the workplace ecosystem.

But let's be honest. Looking at a toxic or
dysfunctional culture can feel overwhelming.
You notice the gossip, the cliques, the lack of
accountability, the disengagement. It's like

staring at a house that's fallen into disrepair, where do you even begin?

You begin with one drawer.

Start Small, Start Now

Change doesn't require grand strategy on day one. You don't need to tear the house down and rebuild it. Just start tidying. One small area. One small act. One clear expectation. One kind word.

It could be as simple as opening a meeting with a moment of gratitude. Shouting out a team member's win. Setting the tone. Showing the team that someone *cares* enough to see them.

That's how you build momentum. That's how you make a house feel like home again. And once that one drawer is clean, the next one is easier. And then the next. Before long, you're seeing real change.

The Myth of Power

You don't need a title to be a leader. Some of the most powerful cultural shifts I've witnessed came from individual contributors, employees without direct reports or lofty job titles, but with immense influence.

Positivity spreads. So does resilience. So does accountability. Culture is viral. Every action is a potential contagion, so what are *you* spreading?

If you see a gap, fill it. If something isn't working, suggest a better way. If someone is consistently being talked over in meetings, advocate for them. Write a job aid if one doesn't exist. Document a process others keep fumbling through. Help someone new find their footing.

Every single act matters.

I've Heard It All Before... and Then I Didn't

There have been moments in my career where I was warned, "That person will never change. Don't bother trying to get their buy-in." But here's the thing, people don't resist change as much as they resist *feeling unseen or powerless*.

When people are brought in early, when they are heard, when they are trusted, they respond.

I've had long-tenured, change-resistant employees become the *biggest champions* of new initiatives. All it took was showing them that the change wasn't happening *to* them, it was happening *with* them. And that they were an important part of the process.

There are no absolutes when it comes to people. We're not robots. We're stories in motion. Don't write someone off just because someone else did.

Ask the Right Questions

Sometimes all it takes to spark transformation is a blank piece of paper and an honest question.

I've handed that paper to team members and asked: "If you could redesign this department from scratch, what would it look like?"

The answers? Thoughtful. Clear. Bold. They weren't asking for the moon. Most of the time, they were asking for fairness, for clarity, for tools to do their job better, for recognition. Basic things that no one had thought to ask them.

Common themes always emerged. Things that could be improved immediately without budget approvals or corporate buy-in, just simple, human-centered changes that showed we were listening.

Communication Isn't Optional

If there's one cultural issue that comes up over and over again, it's the lack of communication.

Time and again, I've seen the fallout from poor communication: confusion, resentment, disengagement. "We didn't know." "Why are we just now hearing about this?" "What does this mean for our team?"

I've been in that seat too, as a leader finding out about a change *after* the team does. It puts you in a defensive position and erodes trust.

Don't let your team be the last to know. If you have information, share it. Be honest when you don't have answers. Give updates even when there's nothing new to report. Silence breeds anxiety. Communication builds confidence.

If metrics are being tracked, sales, bonuses, satisfaction scores, make sure people *know* where they stand. If goals shift, communicate *why*. Give your team a line of sight to success.

Be the person who breaks the cycle of information hoarding.

Appreciation Is a Leadership Tool

If communication builds trust, appreciation reinforces it.

Appreciate out loud. Publicly. Frequently. Not just the "star performers." Everyone. Recognize effort, not just results. Celebrate progress, not just perfection.

Host a pizza lunch. Bring in a veggie tray if that's more your team's speed. Celebrate birthdays. Recognize Customer Service Appreciation Week. And more importantly, *don't let the appreciation end there.*

Create a culture where saying thank you is normal. Where someone going above and beyond doesn't get lost in the noise. And when someone gets it right after weeks of trying? Celebrate the breakthrough.

People shouldn't wonder if they're doing a good job. Let them know.

Culture Lives Between the Meetings

It's easy to think culture is about the big stuff, strategy decks, vision statements, off-sites. But it actually lives in the in-between. The hallway conversations. The lunchroom energy. The way people respond when someone makes a mistake.

Culture is how we treat each other when no one's watching.

It's how we respond to negativity, like I did in that restroom on my first day, met with an exasperated "thank God it's over." I could've leaned into that energy. Asked follow-up questions. Fed the frustration.

But I didn't. I redirected it. Because I've learned: when you don't fuel drama, it fizzles out.

You don't need to police every conversation. But you *can* set the tone. Every moment is a chance to either reinforce the problem, or model the solution.

Let People Grow

Micromanagement kills culture. So does rescuing people from their own learning.

Your job isn't to do the work for them. It's to empower them *to figure it out*. That doesn't mean abandoning them. It means coaching, not controlling. Supporting, not smothering.

I've had team members who had been in roles for years but never truly learned them, because past leaders did everything for them. And while it was a tough adjustment at first, after a few months of patient support and clear expectations, they bloomed.

They finally *understood* their jobs. And they were proud of that. *I* was proud of that.

People want to grow. But they need leaders willing to let them try.

Protect Your Team, And Raise the Bar

Not every team gets the spotlight. Not every department is sales or marketing. If you lead customer service, operations, or other often-overlooked teams, you know exactly what I mean.

You are your team's advocate.

When they're unfairly blamed, protect them. When they're struggling, investigate the why, was it workload, training gaps, lack of clarity? Don't rush to throw people under the bus. Instead, lift the hood and see what's broken.

Sometimes, culture change requires tough decisions. If someone isn't a fit, it's okay to acknowledge that. But let that decision come from care, not convenience.

Lead with honesty. Not ego. Not fear.

The Ripple Will Reach the Shore

Cultural change happens one decision at a time. One boundary set. One conversation handled with compassion. One drawer cleaned.

You may not change an entire system overnight.

But you can change the moment you're in. And when you do that, the next moment becomes easier. That ripple will reach the shore.

Your voice matters.

And every choice you make echoes louder than you think.

This isn't the end of a book. It's the beginning of a movement. A new standard. One that starts with you.

If we get this right, you can be the picture of organizational change in your company. You can be the ember that ignites the fire.

Compassion is currency. Performance and kindness aren't mutually exclusive, they're a lock and key. You can run high-performing teams with empathy, care, and clarity. Your team can outperform others at the same level. Your team can become the standard that others look to.

You can create a psychologically safe space where people speak up without fear. Where they're encouraged to ideate, innovate, and share freely. You can foster diversity from within, because sameness doesn't generate new ideas. The only way to break out of stagnation is to bring in different voices and lived experiences. Great ideas don't come from silos.

Integrity isn't performative. It's deeply ingrained. It shows in how you treat people. In how you make decisions. When your choices are rooted in integrity, they'll be felt. They'll be trusted. And they'll often be the right ones, not just ethically, but strategically.

You'll start to see retention rise. Burnout fade. Engagement deepen. Because people who are respected, resourced, and led with care don't want to leave.

You can be the change. You can lead the change that drives healthy culture.

Ask yourself: *What would your day-to-day feel like if you lived in this kind of culture?* What if your workplace, while it might sound idealistic, actually supported your best self?

It's not out of reach. It's not utopian. It's possible. And it's possible because you are here. Now. Ready to take those small steps forward.

Small Steps, Big Change

So how do you start?

- **Hold space for tough conversations.**

- **Be brave.** Be willing to listen.

- **Help someone rise.** Don't fear losing your place as a leader, real leaders elevate others.

- **Speak up and speak out.** Say what needs to be said, even when it's hard.

- **Bring solutions, not just problems.**

- **Be truthful and self-aware.** Empower your team to do the same.

- **Choose alignment over approval.**

Some people will scoff. I've had managers roll their eyes at my approach, my openness, my willingness to adapt and make change. But when they see the results? They stop second-guessing it.

And if the system you're in refuses to change, don't become stagnant. Sometimes, the bravest thing you can do is walk away, and build something better.

Change won't happen overnight. Even if you're the CEO. But in every meeting, every conversation, every interaction, you have the chance to model the new standard.

Whether you're a team lead or a company president, **you have a voice.** And **you have a choice.**

Creating Your Own Wake of Change

Here's how you begin:

- **Reflect.** Look at the last ten decisions, meetings, and conversations. Were they values-aligned?

- **Audit your leadership.** Do your actions match your principles?

- **Identify a future leader.** Pour into them. Show them what leadership looks like when it's done right.

- **Challenge the mindset.** Don't let toxic behaviors slide. Don't let "the little things" stack.

Let me tell you a story.

There was someone on my team who, when I first stepped into the role, was clearly looking for a way out. You can usually tell when someone is running from something rather than toward something. They had applied for a variety of roles across multiple departments, and while it's true that some people have broad interests, this was different. It was scattershot. Unfocused. And it raised a flag.

So I did what every leader should do, I took the time to get to know them. We built trust over a few months of one-on-one meetings. Once we had that foundation, I spoke honestly with them. I said, "When leaders see someone peppering the job board with applications across unrelated areas, it doesn't come across as ambitious. It comes across as someone trying to escape."

That conversation opened a door.

We talked about their passions, what really lit them up. And from that conversation, two potential paths emerged. Both aligned with leadership.

I created a simple self-assessment for them. A kind of readiness document, asking them to reflect on the core skills they'd need to grow into leadership: *Do you meet this? Exceed it? Still need development?* And I asked them to be honest.

They returned with their completed assessment, and what I saw was both promising and telling. There were strengths, but also blind spots. The kind of blind spots you don't even know you have until someone helps you see them.

So I made it my mission to help them grow.

They were a team lead at the time, so I gave them space to lead. They began holding one-on-ones with the team members in their area. I coached them through those conversations, how to listen, how to guide, how to create positive change. I told them, "If something's confidential, keep it to yourself. These meetings are yours. Own them."

Then I gave them more.

I assigned projects so they could build their project management skills. I asked them to develop business plans and present their ideas. They helped design a knowledge site, a ticketing system, and led meetings. I coached, but I also stepped back, because empowerment requires trust.

Most importantly, I taught them how to lead with compassion and understanding. Not because it's trendy. But because it works.

What happened next? They stopped running from. They started growing toward. Not because they were desperate to leave, but because they were finally aligned with purpose.

That's the wake. That's how it begins.

Lead Without Permission

You don't have to be the CEO. You don't have to be a manager, a team lead, or the head of HR. You don't even need to have it all figured out.

Start anyway.

Because **title doesn't matter. Impact does.**

Be the leader you always needed.

You've likely worked under bad managers. Most of us have. Think back. What did you wish they had done differently? What did you need that they never gave you?

Start there. Change one thing. Even if it's small.

A new standard isn't coming.

It's already here. And it starts with you.

1. Self-Assessment: Leadership Values Check-In

Instructions: Rate each statement on a scale of 1–5.
1 = Strongly Disagree, 5 = Strongly Agree.

#	Statement	Rating (1–5)
1	I lead with empathy, even when under pressure.	
2	I regularly seek and incorporate feedback from my team.	
3	I address conflict directly, calmly, and fairly.	
4	I practice what I preach, even when no one is watching.	
5	I encourage diverse opinions and voices in conversations.	
6	I set clear expectations and follow through on commitments.	
7	I've created a psychologically safe environment for my team.	
8	I know my team's strengths and support their growth.	
9	I stand up for what's right, even if it's not popular.	
10	I value results *and* well-being equally.	
11	I make space for gratitude, even during high-stress times.	
12	I've built trust within my team.	

13	I check my own bias regularly.	
14	I don't avoid difficult conversations, I approach them with care.	
15	I recognize small wins and contributions consistently.	
16	I speak up when I witness injustice or harmful behavior.	
17	I actively create opportunities for others to lead.	
18	I apologize when I'm wrong.	
19	I've cultivated a culture of learning, not blame.	
20	I am the leader I once needed.	

Scoring Guide:

- 80–100: You're a values-driven leader on the right path.

- 60–79: You're aware and evolving, keep building.

- Below 60: Time to reflect, recalibrate, and recommit.

2. Blank Page: Team Values Worksheet

Use the next page to co-create your team's values.

Team Values Brainstorming Prompts:

- What behaviors do we want to be known for?

- What values will guide our decision-making under pressure?

- How do we want people to feel when they work with us?

3. Culture Health Check

Answer honestly based on what you see, feel, and hear. **Yes / No / Unsure**

1. Are communication channels clear, transparent, and consistent?

2. Have you or others witnessed workplace bullying or harassment?

3. Is gossip a noticeable part of the culture?

4. Do employees often work unpaid overtime just to keep up?

5. Are workloads fairly distributed?

6. Is pay equitable across gender, race, and role?

7. Do the benefits (healthcare, time off, mental health) support wellbeing?

8. Are employees encouraged to speak up without fear?

9. Are diverse voices heard and elevated?

10. Does the organization claim to be people-centered... but act otherwise?

Score:

- Mostly "Yes" = Culture is on track.

- Mostly "No" or "Unsure" = Signals of deeper systemic issues worth exploring.

4. Checklist: Everyday Leadership Actions That Create Culture

Mark these when they've become a part of how you lead, not just a one-time effort.

Action	Embedded in My Culture? (✓)
Start meetings with gratitude or appreciation	
Acknowledge someone's effort in front of others	
Ask for team feedback on a decision	
Share personal growth moments to model vulnerability	
Facilitate open discussions without judgment	
Check in with someone who's been quiet or withdrawn	
Celebrate small wins, not just big ones	
Ask "What do you need?" instead of making assumptions	
Set boundaries and encourage others to do the same	
Speak up when something feels unjust	
Pause before reacting to tension or criticism	
Recognize and reduce unnecessary meetings or pressure	
Encourage time off and model it yourself	
Say "thank you" more often	
Correct behavior without shaming	
Allow space for team-led decisions	
Encourage mentorship and peer coaching	
Create rituals of connection (morning check-ins, gratitude boards)	

Model emotional intelligence	
Lead with consistency, not chaos	

5. The Wake We Leave – Leader's Pledge

I pledge to lead with courage, not control. To see the humanity in others, and honor it in how I lead. I will challenge injustice, uplift voices, and foster safety. I will question systems that harm, even when I've benefited from them. I will not let silence become complicity. I will build with kindness, speak with integrity, and act with clarity.

I am the wake I leave behind. And I choose to make it one of healing, growth, and hope.

Signed:

_____

Date:

_____

About the Author

Kim Eckels is a passionate leadership advocate, transformational change agent, and lifelong champion for equity and kindness in the workplace. With a Master of Science in Leadership and Management and more than two decades of experience spanning technical support, customer experience, operations, and team development, Kim has walked the walk, rising from service roles to senior leadership through grit, integrity, and a belief in the power of people.

Her work blends strategy with heart, consistently building psychologically safe cultures, improving onboarding systems, and mentoring others into their own leadership potential. As a speaker, writer, and facilitator, Kim leads with empathy, guided by the belief that performance and compassion aren't opposites, they're partners.

When she's not leading change, Kim can be found walking with her dog, restoring her spirit in nature, or dreaming up her next big idea. *The Wake We Leave* is her call to action for leaders ready to ditch the performative playbook and embrace a more human, values-driven standard.

www.ingramcontent.com/pod-product-compliance
Lightning Source LLC
LaVergne TN
LVHW052037080426
835513LV00018B/2358